# Storm Within Skin

Gracie Borjas

BookLeaf Publishing

India | USA | UK

Presentation by *BookLeaf Publishing*

Web: www.bookleafpub.com

E-mail: info@bookleafpub.com


ISBN: 9789358315967

First edition 2022

# DEDICATION

Jesse- I swallowed the butterfly.

# Shadow Dream

The shadow continues its lava like flow,
easing its way down in a forlorn path.
While the shadow's path is forlorn,
its destination is me.
From the bottom of a soul I do not own,
I pray to a god I doubt.
I pray an invocation thick with faith I do not
carry;
A belief I've long outgrown.
Through the sheer intensity of my shrilling,
meaningless benediction, the raven shadow
begins to rescind its enveloping promise.

# Broken Wings

I'm like a moth
with broken wings
and tattered dreams.
What was once solid,
has now liquefied and
evaporated.
Leaves me with nothing.
My hopes,
My dreams,
now all a figment of my imagination.
Once was here,
Now they're gone.
Broken wings
and tattered dreams.
No possible way to fly.
Nothing to fly towards.
Arise sweet butterfly!
Arise!
Come to the light,
and bring a dream
to humble reality.

# White Butterfly

White butterfly-
Come play with me.
Show me your virginal wings
against my scarred face.
Come lay your wings
on my tear soaked eyelids.
Come give me gentle kisses
on my forehead.
Let me know you live!
Let me know you breathe!
White butterfly-
show me your pretty smile
and your impossibly real,
glittering personality.
White butterfly-
bring me a sprig of oleander,
magical and deadly.
Bring me a scent.
The scent of sweet death.
The irony is thick on my tongue.
White butterfly-
teach me your love.

# Wrapped In Satin

I'm wrapped in satin
in an attempt to make some part of me delicate.
Paint my portrait with gentle strokes
and make me soft.
I've been hardened,
an insensitive likeness of a woman.
I'm wrapped in satin
to be beautiful,
to shield myself from the ugliness of the world.
The luscious cloth is all of me
that is delicate.

# Center

I gaze absently out the window
as the mother tells her son to spell,
"center,"
and I wonder
where mine is.

# Children of the Night

We are the children of the night.
Wanderers of the splendid darkness,
tamers of the time untouched by day.
We walk silently among its comfort.
We are the chosen,
called by the lack of light.
We, the children of the night,
roam free in the unspoken womb
that cradles us.
It keeps us here.
We are the children of the night,
endlessly seeking dawn,
prevailing into darkness;
not finding the ray of light we crave.
The children of the light
is who were are,
and who we are,
we cannot overcome.

# Fire Inside

I've been lit from the inside,
a fire burning within.
From somewhere deep beneath
the bellows of my belly.
Hot, hot like lava.
The heat I emanate
can burn down buildings,
destroy cities, and families.
If I give into its strength...
If I should fuel the fire
or allow it to manifest...
My fire will destroy you at the sight of its
flames.
Should you choose to tempt the monster,
have faith- I will win.
You will not succeed
in extinguishing my fire.

# My One

When he hears a song in the morning,
I have it stuck in my head all day.
When he's upset,
I feel his anger
twisting in my gut.
I know we are more than in love.
Even when he is not here,
I feel his tug on my heartstrings.
The sweet pitter patter of his name beats in my
chest.
My boisterous voice bellows in his.
He makes me brave-
makes me believe I can face the day when my
soul is weary.
His smile is the sun
and he loves me enough to let
my brooding moon glow through
the darkness inside me.
Encourages me to shine through the clouds.
He loves me more than I know what to do with,
and I cannot wrap my mind around its enormity.
His heart is fragile in my hands.
I hold it like it's glass and I swear to tend to it
like magic blooming in the midnight garden.

He is my one.

# Take Me

I try
      again
         again
            and again
to run from myself
but my house is too small
        There aren't enough places to
hide.
My cries rattle the windows of my house, tears
threatening flood damage.
I've consumed so much darkness that
        I have become the night.
When will the sky take me?

# Exaltation

I refuse to set my soul on fire for him
Because he refuses to exalt me.
I've shown you my birth chart
I've shown you I am worth worshipping.
Point to your chest and tell me
Your heart is my home.
Carve my initials into your brainstem.
I am not requesting entrance.
With a voice that sounds like it's been gargling
gasoline,
I am announcing my presence.

# Choke

I will not break myself down to be more
palatable for you.
I will stay whole
and you can choke.
You can be the beggar digging through garbage,
trying to find the meatiest parts to satiate your
hunger.
You will starve before me.
I no longer bend, break, or bow to the will of
your weak mind.
I do not seek to appease your appetite.
I. do. not. care. if. you. choke.

# Song of Sorrow

Rain dances on my window;
words sing a song in my head.
I can't find the tune to put it together.
The silence brings more words.
Somewhere in the distance, the phone rang.
Is it you, calling my name?
My muse has abandoned me.
Catalyst is my middle name.
Sing a song of silence.
Not within my head.
Bless the wicked flame;
kiss the crystal sky.
Break the neurosis
of a rainy day.
I long to sing my song of sorrow.
I hum a tune,
unfamiliar, yet known.
It dries the thoughts
my mind wishes to have bled.
My song of sorrow
has no end.

# Ambiance

Maggots manifest malignantly
on my novice,
youthful mind.
Eating, bleeding,
and feeding.
Rotting my innocence away.
Cutting through my pores.
Effecting my physical being.
I push it onto you.
No longer my
masochistic agenda.
You now possess this rancid,
tumescent brain of noodles
which drip of acidity.
I look within you
and see the pestilence I passed your soul.
I think for a moment...
I might want it back, but
then I realized it's better yours than mine.
Keep the filth.
Let it rot your mind.
Keep me at peace.
My selfishness allows me to go no further
with the poison
I passed.

# Time to Say Goodbye

When it's time to say goodbye,
I want to know
our time was well spent.
When it's time to say goodbye,
I want you to remember all the
things we had
and the things that made us laugh.
When it's time to say goodbye,
I want it to be short-lived
and simply a product of habit.
When it's time to say goodbye,
you should know,
I will keep you in my heart.
Always.

# Puppets

What insignificant, disgusting
little puppets
we are.
Dancing and prostituting
without a care in the world.
Parading ourselves as joyous,
mindless, soulless wonders.
We have no meaning.
We are the disgusting little puppets,
which care of nothing
but to frolic in our own
bacterial waste,
living meaningless,
sex driving lives
in a paradise lost.

# Corner of the Sky

There are cobwebs
in my corner of the sky.
No one visits anymore.
The lonely legacy
been left to me.
My dreams have fallen onto the dirt.
My corner of the sky,
aflame with despair.
The recycled heart behind it
is enough to put me to shame.
The effort for love
is enough to make anyone empty of all emotion.
Letting go of the center of life,
maybe it will come naturally.
Here in my corner of the sky,
the desolation
demolished my delirium.

# Underneath

The darkness is underneath,
buried deep, deep in your sea.
It pitches you
dark and deep.
It's forever yours to keep.
It's beating you,
keeping you down.
Dark and lonely,
and I can't keep going.
Nothing there to heal.
All of it- living to kill.
Eating your soul;
taking your life.
The darkness you feel
is so very real.

# Harmony

Harmony sits at her table
drinking her afternoon tea,
quietly reading the newspaper.
Silence comes in and speaks
gentle words into her ear.
Harmony is at peace with her world,
until
Chaos rears her rambunctious head.
Silence and Chaos quarrel.
Chaos leaves Harmony's kitchen,
leaving her with Silence
once again.

# I Sing

The deep huskiness of my voice
is vibrantly absorbed into the microphone.
At last, I speak.
No, I sing!
A songbird,
free in an azure sky.
At last, I sing.
No words are heard;
then, I sing.
Sweet and strong,
this voice of mine.
Thick and sweet as honey.
Sweet symphony of poetry
strung together by music.
Changing them from words to lyrics,
in this powerful, beautiful
voice of mine.
And, I sing.
No words to describe the succulence
in a voice like this.
And, I sing!
The voice I want,
the voice I crave
I own.
And, I sing.

I sing.

# Naked

I've been stripped naked
of all emotion
Revealed to the world
how I really feel.
My nakedness
leaves my heart aching.
I'm empty.
Bare.
Stripped naked.
You've seen all I am;
there's nothing left of me.
I'm naked.
Stripped bare,
to you.

# Pen My Words

I pen my words
to pen my soul-
to be understood by someone,
to reach a kindred spirit,
to release onto the earth my true form.
To divide my reality from my fallacy
and lies.
To seek the truth beyond my sight.
To tell the world a story.
To sail across a milky sky,
to melt the arctic caps.
To live a life through words.
I pen my words
to pen myself
and my purpose.

www.ingramcontent.com/pod-product-compliance
Lightning Source LLC
LaVergne TN
LVHW051251200726

843510LV00011B/1799

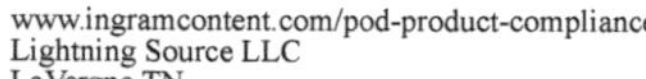